The Land of the Taffeta Dawn

NATALIA BELTING

The Land of the Taffeta Dawn

illustrated by JOSEPH LOW

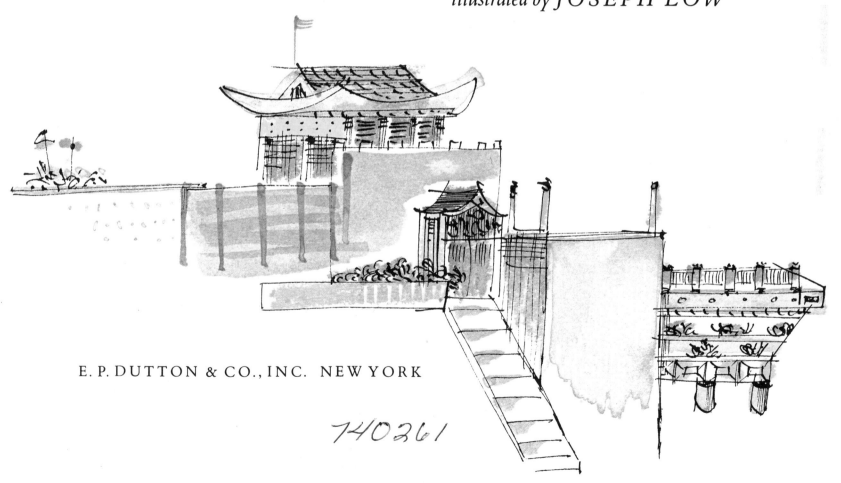

E. P. DUTTON & CO., INC. NEW YORK

The Northmen who harassed England and all the coastlands of Europe in the eighth and ninth and tenth centuries were also traders and founders of kingdoms. By the time Alfred was king of England, these men had established a trading kingdom at the head of the Dnieper River that the Slavic-speaking natives called the Kingdom of the Russ—that is, the Kingdom of the Northmen. Vikings settled along the Dnieper, and traded on it and the Don and Volga rivers to Samarkand, the western end of the mountain-and-desert trails that led to the great empire of T'ang China— the fabulous land of silk.

While their swift dragon-ships
Strake frost-cold seas
Helmed straight as the gannet flies
To Scotch, to Irish shores,
To English coves,
French river towns,
And shimmering coastlands
Warmed by the Middle Sea,
—Crews bent on plundering—,

Norse merchant-ships
Lumber all the seas,
And Northmen follow
Down the Dnieper, Don,
The Volga;
Ferry sables, honey, amber,
Wax to trade in Samarkand
For silk and porcelain

And for tales
About the Land of Silk
To the east
In the taffeta dawn
Where magic looms
Weave gauze and peacock net,
Brocade and samite—fairy silks,
And enchanters pot
Translucent bowls
And cups and plates
From snow-white clay.

Nine roads
Lead to the Land of Silk,

Cross the ice roof at the top of the world,
Cross the singing sands that whirl in the midst of the Gobi,
Cross Lop Nor, salt-paved, burning,
The haunt of the wailing, restless ghosts;

Nine roads
Pebbled with agates and garnets
And spinel rubies,
Ochred red and yellow
By streams that wash them

Lead to Ch'ang-an,
Capital city
Of the Land of Silk,
Of the Empire of T'ang.

– The Gate of Spring Brightness,
The Gate of Gold Light,
The Red Phoenix gate –

Nine gates breach walls
Of ashlar and brick,

Open on elm-shaded streets,
Canals, the Curving Stream,
Parks and pavilions,

And beyond the city,
North, above the city
On Dragonshead highlands
Rainbow mists, five-colored clouds
Screen the emperor's palace
From common view.

Such wares as they sell
At the city markets
Can hardly be told:

Damasks, and cottons
Like sunrise clouds;

Purple skins,
Red-felt boots;

Porcelain dishes
And bottles and stoves;

Whatever one can imagine
Is made out of jade, and for sale:
Hairpins, bridle-clasps, spoons,
Carved jade incense clocks;
There is even jade powdered,
In liquid, for drinking
To achieve a long life,

And cages of jade
For talking birds.

There are perfumes,
Peppercorns, saffron;
Mouse-catching cedar-wood cats;
Puppets;
Otters of pine that dive after fish.

And though it isn't for sale,
There's a life-sized mechanical beggar
That wanders some days
Around by the shops,
Extending his bowl,
Crying "Alms, alms,"
Till a merchant or trader or buyer, someone
Tosses coins in.

Whoever has business
With the Emperor of T'ang,
Or gifts for him,
Petitions, requests,
Has to attend a levee at dawn.

Winter and summer,
Autumn and spring, the emperor's audiences
Are always at dawn.

Ambassadors, scholars,
Relatives, friends,
Whoever they are,
Go up the blue-cobbled road,
The Dragon-tail way,
Between red-painted pavilions,
Gardens and groves and pools,
Past Honeybush Hall where the library is,
And the Tower for Observing the Heavens,

Pass between the household troops,
All scarlet-shirted
With taffeta tabards
Embroidered in leaping wild horses,

Bow to the emperor
In his pearl-tassled cap
Of state, his furs. If it's spring,
He is wearing garments of kingfisher blue...

So it is said, but no one can see;
He is hid by clouds of incense swirling
Even as he speaks.

But clerks set his words down
On paper or silk, with pen or with brush,
To be posted for reading.

With the sun rising,
The audience ends.

Before winter breaks
They celebrate spring
With the Feast of Lanterns
In the first month.

They hang out lanterns made
Of paper, silk,
Parrot-shaped, and lantern-cockatoos
With beaks that open, close,
While lighted dragonflies sail from bamboo poles
And peacock lanterns made of fog silk
Spread their tails.

Strolling, men and women,
Children too, trail lanterns set on tiny wheels,
Play catch at dusk with gimbaled lamp-balls.

A thousand white-silk lanterns strung,
Ten thousand lantern moons
Confuse the Curving Stream.

Lamp trees
Twice in height the tallest man,
With a thousand porcelain saucers
Burning fragrant oil
Stand by temple, mansion gates;
And through the night,
Through the Hour of the Fowl,
The Hour of the Dog,
The Hour of the Pig,

Fireworks, flame flowers,
Circle, wheel, bloom
Above the Street of Heaven,
The Street of the Pine,
The Azure gate,
Great Goose pagoda,
Bloom above Ch'ang-an
Till dawn.

A woman was empress once of T'ang—
Not born of a royal family,
Quite common, but she married the emperor,
Made herself ruler when he died.

Mad Empress Wu, they called her.
One winter's day
She ordered all the flowers to bloom at once
In the snow.
(We have heard
They did.)

Another day she said that henceforth
No one might be appointed
A court minister, or governor, or mayor,
Or ennobled
Unless he was a poet.

Now, in T'ang, boys go to school for years,
Sunrise to sunset,
Learning to write,
Learning to be poets,

So they may pass the state examinations,
Wear blue silk robes
Or purple ones, ride
In carriages with vermilion wheels,
Never have to serve as soldiers,
And perhaps, some day
Be made princes, dukes.

Poets, when they have passed
The examinations, receive the title
Of Advanced Gentlemen,

Celebrate with picnics
In the Apricot garden,

Write their names, and poems
With pine-soot ink
Perfumed with pomegranate bark, or musk,
With sheep's-wool brushes,
Or fox, or wolf-hair brushes,
Or mouse-whisker brushes

On the walls
Of Great Goose pagoda.

In the fourth month
Tree peonies bloom everywhere…

Masses of bloom in gardens
Stand shaded
By tiffany tilts
Of embroidered silk;

Foot pagodas,
Pavilions,
Kiosks, walls;

Border rillets,
Ponds and canals.

Princes, dukes,
All the Nine ranks of the nobility,
The emperor, empress—
—Vermilion silk robes—
—Carnation jade pendants—

Rich and old,
Poor and young,
Afoot, on horse,
In carriages, chairs, at dawn
Wander wherever the peonies are.

They crowd the flower market
For peony plants and blooms.

The prices are hard to believe:
A hundred pieces of damask…
(A hundred days' weaving,
And more than the price of a horse)
For a single fine flower.
Cheap flowers cost five pieces of silk.

They call the fifth month
Wicked, evil, pestilential.

The sky brasses,
The yellow earth dries.

Then they petition the Rain Dragon.

Villagers make clay dragons,
Cast them in the river.

Townsfolk shut the city's south gates,
Open the north gates wide
So the Rain Dragon can come in,

Burn paper dragons
Or dragons carved
Of aromatic white sandalwood.

But there are those, in T'ang,
Who say dragons cannot make rain,
They say no matter if men call them gods,
Pray to them,
Dragons are only dragons.

In winter workmen
Saw blocks of ice off mountain rivers,
Fill ice houses, pits.

In summer palaces and mansions
Are cooled by breezes
Fanned across the ice.

Watermelons, cantaloupes
Are kept in pits of mountain snow,
Served in jade bowls, or porcelain,
Set in ice,
With bits of ice for eating.

Wine boats float round
Ice-cooled garden streams
With puppets on them pouring wine,
And puppet dancers dancing
To tunes of puppet bands

While burning incense
In bronze or silver censing baskets
Keeps insects distant.

Gold peaches ripen
Along the Yellow Canal from the river
To the park of the Curving Stream
The seventh month at Ch'ang-an.

Blue-feathered kingfishers
Hunt among crimson lotuses
While hundred-hued dragonflies
Skim white and yellow water lilies
And cocket finches frolic
In rock-tossed crystal spray.

At the full moon the dead return
From the Nine Streams,
From the Terrace of the Night
To visit and feast with their families

At tables set by open garden gates
With silk-gauze cloths and scented candles
And piled with food and gifts:

…Hemp-seed cakes,
New millet, pickled melon,
Cane sugar shaped into tigers,
Elephants, and tiny men…

…Peonies and peach blooms,
Skirts and shirts and boots and caps,
Kites and skiffs and sampans,
Peacocks, turtles, toads, and goldfish
All fashioned out of paper, silk,
All cricket-size.

At temples nuns and monks
Set out food, spread out gifts,
Burn candles, incense
For the ghosts who have no families,
The hungry and the orphaned ghosts.

Traders from T'ang
Will always buy horses.
They have bought five, ten thousand at once.

The price of a horse is fifty pieces of silk.
They will pay it.

We have heard
Three-quarter million horses graze
In the imperial pastures: war horses;
Dwarf horses for ladies' pleasure carts;
Ponies for playing the Turkish game, polo.

And the hundred tiger-marked dancing horses
They say are offspring of mares
Coupled with dragons.

On the Holiday of a Thousand Autumns,
The fifth day of the eighth month,
The dancing horses are caparisoned
In embroidered saffron silk,
Bridled with silver and gold,
Manes plaited with jade and pearls.

The court orchestra plays
And they dance, these horses of dragons,
Atop a wood platform three storeys high.

They dance, one at a time, on a divan
Upholstered in silk
And never misstep.

Traders from T'ang
Will pay the very best prices
For horses.

Before winter's cold comes,
And the deep snow,
The emperor goes to his Palace of Beautiful Flowers,
And the hot sulphur springs on Mount Li
Where the mineral lakes
Have miniature mountains carved
Of lapis lazuli.

And the court goes with him.
His consort and concubines,
Three thousand maids of honor and palace women,
Little girls and dancing girls,
Musicians and poets,
And the household troops,

Leaving the Great Shining palace
North of Ch'ang-an slumbering
Like a hibernating dragon
In the drifting snow.

West from T'ang
Beyond the damask twilight,
West from Samarkand
And north
On rivers and seasteads

Norse merchant-ships
Lumber laden
With Eastern wares
For kings and counts
And knights and ladies,
And fairy tales to tell
Around the hearth-fires
Winter nights
Of the land that lies
East of the sun,
The land of the taffeta dawn.

NATALIA BELTING is assistant professor of history at the University of Illinois, where she received her undergraduate and graduate degrees. Miss Belting's interest in historical research has resulted in numerous books for young people, told in freely flowing poetry. The list includes *Calendar Moon* (an ALA Notable Book) and *The Sun Is a Golden Earring* (a Caldecott Medal Honor Book), both illustrated by Bernarda Bryson. Along with her historical pursuits, Miss Belting is interested in gardening, cooking, and excavating artifacts of the Illinois Indians from her property in Urbana.

JOSEPH LOW is an alumnus of the University of Illinois and the Art Students League. His distinctive graphic style has been honored by the American Institute of Graphic Arts, the Society of Illustrators, and the Art Directors Club. Mr. Low's illustrations for *The Land of the Taffeta Dawn* are "meant to evoke two vastly different though contemporary peoples: Viking toughness and vigor; Chinese subtlety and elaboration— both richly inventive, each clearly expressive." The illustrations were drawn in pen line, combined with Pelikan inks and soft oil crayon for the color. Mr. Low now divides his time between the operation of his own Eden Hill Press and book illustration. He and his wife spend winters in the Virgin Islands and summers on Martha's Vineyard.

The text and display type are set in photo Bembo. The book is printed by offset.